Wētāpunga

The biggest wētā in the world

Thank you to the Ngāti Manuhiri Settlement Trust for graciously allowing this book to go ahead. In particular Mook Hohneck, Ringi Brown and Vern Rosieur for their guidance with the project. As the kaitiaki, or guardians, of Te Hauturu-o-Toi (Little Barrier) their involvement was fundamental to the success of the breeding programme. By allowing breeding pairs of wētāpunga to be taken from Te Hauturu-o-Toi, the last place in the world where they could be found, the trust has ensured the future of this unique arthropod; a taonga, a treasure.

Thank you to the team at Auckland Zoo, especially Don McFarlane (Curator of Ectotherms) and Jane Healy (Communications Manager) for their support in the production of this book. This project would not have been possible without their help in verifying the facts and supplying the stunning photographs of this weird and wonderful arthropod. To find out more about the extraordinary wētāpunga, and Auckland Zoo's wētāpunga conservation programme, visit www.aucklandzoo.co.nz

Published in 2025 by David Bateman Ltd,
Unit 2/5 Workspace Drive, Hobsonville,
Auckland 0618, New Zealand
www.batemanbooks.co.nz
ISBN: 978-1-77689-126-9

A catalogue record for this book is available from the National Library of New Zealand.

Book design: Jemma Moreira
Printed in China by Toppan Leefung Printing Ltd

Aotearoa has been home to this extraordinary arthropod for over 80 million years.

A very, very long time.

During that time, dinosaurs came and went, but our amazing wētāpunga managed to survive.

FUN FACT

Wētāpunga are one of the biggest insects in the world!

Wētāpunga are an endemic species, which means they are only found in Aotearoa.

You won't see anything quite like them anywhere else in the world.

Wētāpunga is a reo Māori word. The name refers to the impressive size of the arthropod, and reflects both the real weight of the wētāpunga, and the symbolic weight or importance it plays in the ecosystem.

Their scientific name is *Deinacrida heteracantha*, which means 'terrible cricket' or 'mighty locust'.

Neither of those names makes them sound very attractive or friendly, and lots of people do think they are ugly and scary . . .

but others think they are beautiful, gentle giants.

Some people might think that wētāpunga could hurt you.

They do look quite fearsome with their

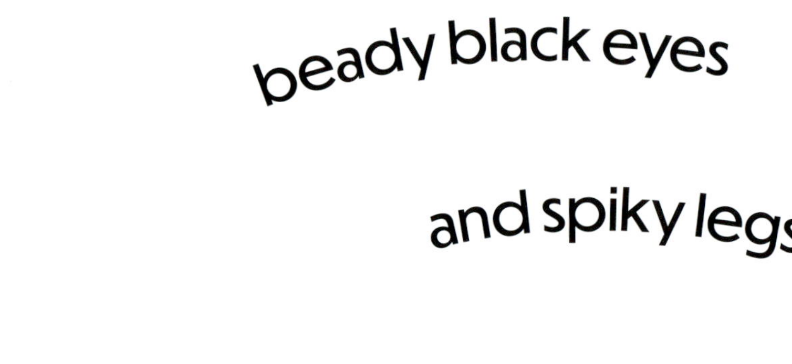

long antennae,

beady black eyes

and spiky legs

but wētāpunga don't sting or scratch.

FUN FACT

Although they can bite, wētāpunga are actually quite harmless. If you leave them alone, they will leave you alone.

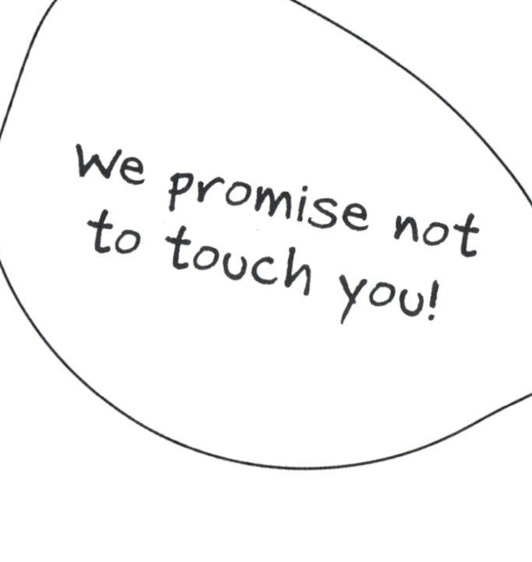

Adult female wētāpunga are heavier than males and have a long spike at the back of their body, which looks a lot like a stinger but isn't. It is a tube called an ovipositor, and she uses it to lay her eggs in the ground.

During the day, wētāpunga hide under loose bark, in plants such as nīkau or ponga or in the cavities of trees like pōhutukawa or māhoe (whiteywood).

They are mostly nocturnal creatures, which means they are active at night.

They emerge from their hiding places when it is dark, so don't try and look for them if it is a full moon!

Wētāpunga don't have a nose like we do — they breathe through holes (called spiracles) on the sides of their bodies.

They have palps by their jaws, which do the job of tasting and smelling.

Their ears are not on their heads, but below the knee joints on their front legs.

They can grow up to 100mm long.

What are you doing with that?
Just testing my knees for ears!
INSECTS R COOL

Wētāpunga don't have a backbone like you or me.

Instead, they have an exoskeleton. This hard outer casing (made of chitin) supports and protects them, like a suit of armour.

They moult as they grow, which means they shed their existing exoskeleton to make way for a new one of the right size.

When wētāpunga are ready to moult, they find a good place to shed the old exoskeleton.

They don't want to be out in the open as they are vulnerable when moulting, but they do need a bit of room to remove the old casing.

This process is called ecdysis.

I am ready
to shed
my skin!
Yuck!
Do I really
need to see
that?

The outer casing splits along the back to reveal the new exoskeleton underneath.

This new casing is soft and pale to begin with, but after a few hours it hardens and gets darker.

The stage between each moult is called an instar. After hatching from the egg, a wētāpunga is said to be in its first instar.

When it moults, it is then in its second instar.

When it moults again, it is in its third instar, and so on.

A wētāpunga goes through 10 instars over a space of nearly two years.

It is then fully grown and doesn't moult again.

Wētāpunga are mainly herbivorous, which means they prefer to eat plants and leaves.

They munch on fresh leaves, especially māhoe, coprosma and hebe, but will occasionally have a meal of a smaller insect.

Wētāpunga eat their old exoskeleton after moulting. It is full of essential nutrients needed to help them grow and develop.

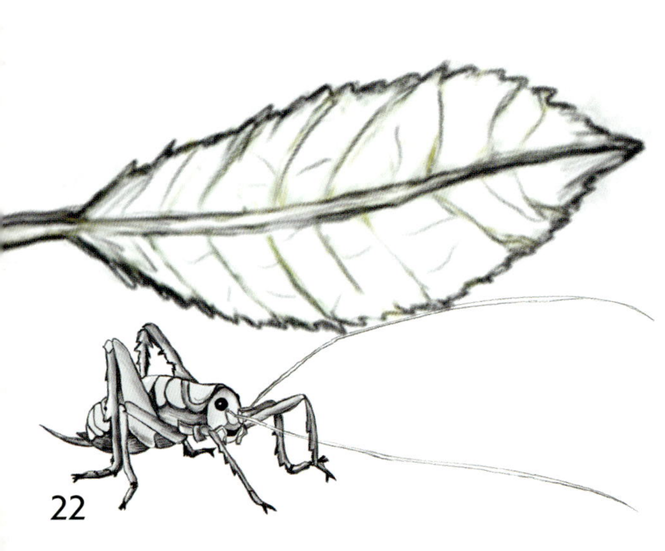

Young wētāpunga are good at jumping, but adults are too heavy to jump. In fact, they are one of the heaviest insects in the world.

Female wētāpunga weigh around 40g, which is even heavier than a mouse.

The heaviest ever recorded was a female wētāpunga carrying eggs. She weighed just over 70g – about as much as 65 jellybeans!

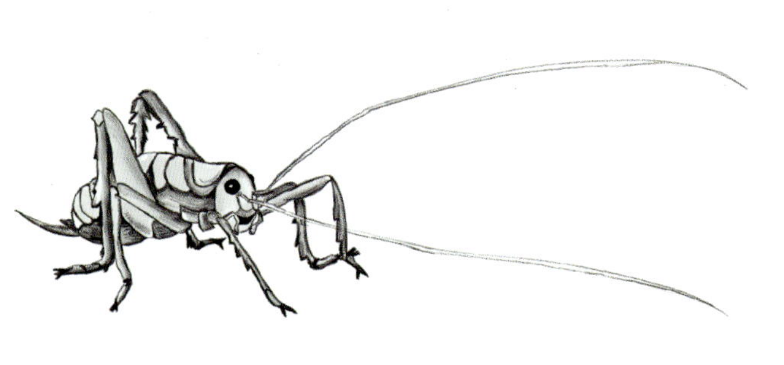

After the final moult, wētāpunga are fully mature and ready to mate.

During her adult life, which is around 9 to 12 months, a female wētāpunga can lay hundreds of eggs.

That is a lot of babies (called nymphs), and you would think that Aotearoa would be overrun with them, but

many,

many,

many

nymphs are eaten by predators.

Wētāpunga are flightless, stingless, heavy and can't run very fast, which makes them easy prey for introduced mammals such as rats, cats, stoats and hedgehogs.

They also have a strong and distinctive smell (which some think rather smelly), so it is easy for predators with a good sense of smell to find them. Their best form of defence is to stay hidden.

If a hungry predator does sniff them out, they raise their spiky legs and make a hissing noise to ward the predator off.

Wētāpunga can also bite or strike with their legs – but they don't stand a chance against the sharp teeth of a hedgehog or stoat.

Before settlers arrived in Aotearoa, the balance of nature was stable.

Wētāpunga were eaten by other native nocturnal creatures, such as tuatara, spiders, kiwi, ruru and bats, but the wētāpunga population could handle these original predators.

With the arrival of settlers bringing new creatures into the country, the balance changed.

When the first settlers from Polynesia arrived in the late 1200s, they brought kiore (Polynesian rats) with them as a source of food.

The kiore soon roamed free and found that wētāpunga were an easy, tasty (and highly nutritious) meal.

When Europeans arrived in the 1700s, they brought cats with them to eat any pesky brown or black rats hidden on the ships.

The cats and the rats soon ran wild and discovered that wētāpunga were an

easy,
tasty,
crispy meal.

More Europeans arrived, bringing hedgehogs and rabbits to remind them of home. The rabbits and hedgehogs ran free. The hedgehogs thought that wētāpunga were an

easy,
tasty,
crispy,
crunchy meal.

The rabbits didn't eat wētāpunga, but they ate the grass meant for sheep and cows.

So . . .

in the late 1800s, stoats and ferrets were brought in to eat the rabbits. They did eat some of the rabbits, but they also discovered that wētāpunga were much easier to catch!

They were an

easy,

tasty,

crispy,

crunchy,

munchy meal.

Around the same time, possums were brought over from Australia to start a fur trade. The possums were (and still are) a huge problem in Aotearoa.

They eat the native plants and berries, birds' eggs, chicks, bats, our huge endemic snail, the *Powelliphanta*, and our precious wētāpunga.

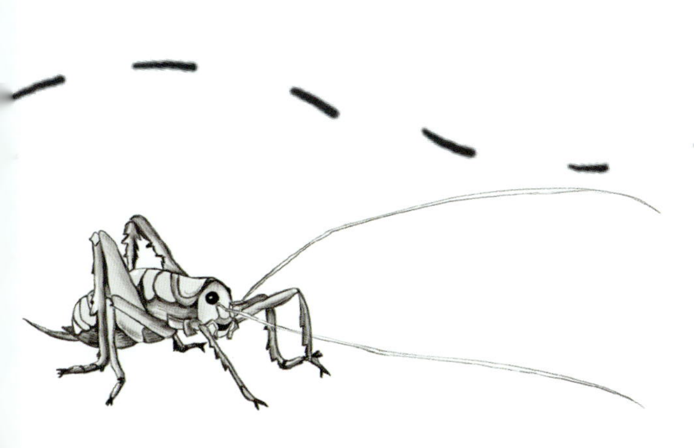

The problem is wētāpunga just smell too good and are highly nutritious.

They don't stand a chance of surviving with all the introduced animals wanting to eat them.

Whether you think them ugly and scary, or beautiful and extraordinary, we should be proud to have one of the heaviest, strangest and most ancient insects as our very own. They are a taonga, a treasure; we must not let them die out.

The last wētāpunga sighted on mainland Aotearoa was in the 1880s. From then on, the only place you could find them in the wild was on Te Hauturu-o-Toi (Little Barrier Island).

In the early 2000s, Auckland's Butterfly Creek started a wētāpunga breeding programme, using pairs from Te Hauturu-o-Toi.

A few years later, with the blessing from the Ngāti Manuhiri Settlement Trust (the kaitiaki, or guardians, of Te Hauturu-o-Toi), Auckland Zoo joined the project, with fantastic results. Between 2014–2024, they bred and released more than 7000 wētāpunga!

This is really helping to save the species, and they can now be found on eight predator-free islands in the waters of Te Moananui-ā-Toi/ Tīkapa Moana (Hauraki Gulf) and Pēwhairangi (Bay of Islands).

There are 11 species of giant wētā in Aotearoa (wētāpunga are the biggest) and most of these are endangered.

The Department of Conservation has a giant wētā recovery plan. This plan encourages moving endangered species to new homes that are free of mammal predators.

Moving giant wētā from places with predators to predator-free habitats is helping to save these extraordinary insects.

It is also helping with forest regeneration. They return nutrients to the soil through their gigantic, ginormous poos; one of the biggest poos produced by an insect!

There are lots of simple things that WE can do to help protect other wētā species.

Make sure gardens and school grounds have places for wētā to hide, such as rocky walls and wood piles.

Keep parts of your garden wild to attract native animals.

Plant native trees and shrubs like māhoe, coprosma and hebe — plants that wētā like to eat. Put a fence around those areas to keep out hedgehogs. Make sure the fence has no gaps and goes into the soil to prevent predators from crawling under it.

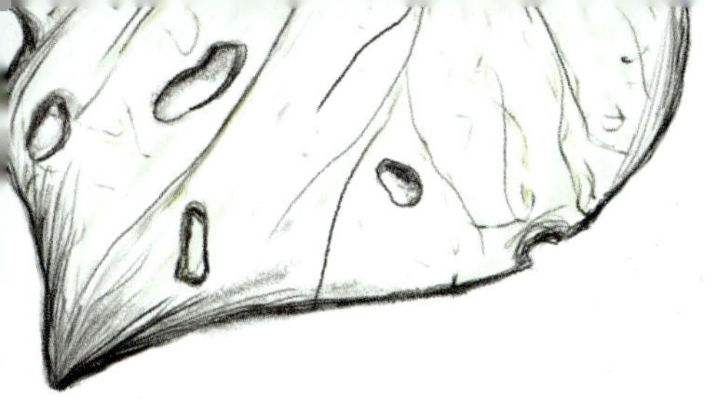

Use natural, chemical-free pesticides and fertilisers.

If you have a pet cat, you can train it to be happy indoors or keep it inside at night. You can also put up a cat net or create a cat patio, which limits the area in which your cat can prowl. See www.spca.nz for further advice and ideas.

If there is a wild cat in your neighbourhood, tell your local council and they should be able to catch it.

Rats are a pest and eat more than just wētā — they also eat the eggs and chicks of our native birds. You can set humane traps in your garden to catch and despatch those pesky rats.

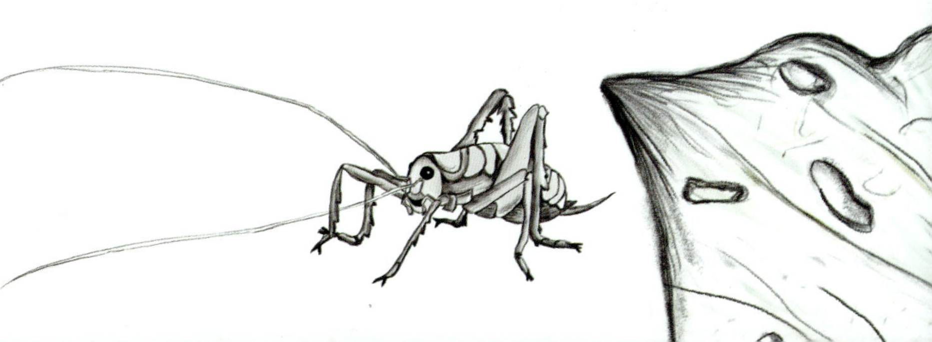

I know it wasn't you or me who brought new predators to Aotearoa all those years ago.

I know it wasn't you or me who caused this problem — but we are the ones who can fix it.

Wētāpunga and other wētā need our help.

Let's do our bit to protect them and stop this amazing ancient creature from becoming extinct.

GLOSSARY

Arthropod: An invertebrate with an exoskeleton, jointed legs and a segmented body.

Chitin: A structural polysaccharide made from chains of modified glucose. It is found in the exoskeleton of insects, some hard structures in fish and invertebrates and the cell walls of fungi.

Ecdysis: Ecdysis is the process of an arthropod moulting or shedding its exoskeleton.

Ectotherm: A creature that depends on external heat sources to regulate its temperature. Their body temperature changes with the temperature of the environment.

Endemic: A creature or plant that is natural or native to a specific place or region.

Exoskeleton: An exoskeleton is a hard outer layer (made of chitin) that protects, covers and supports the body of a creature such as an insect, crustacean or mollusc.

Extinct: If a creature is extinct, it means it's no longer in existence; there are none left in the world.

Instar: The developmental stage of an arthropod between each moult.

Moult: The process of shedding skin, hair, fur or exoskeleton, making way for new growth.

Nymph: The juvenile form of some invertebrates, including wētāpunga.

Ovipositor: The tube-like organ that a female wētāpunga uses to lay eggs in damp soil.

Palps: A pair of sensory organs next to the mouth of a wētāpunga that help it taste and smell food.

Spiracles: Tiny holes on the exoskeleton of a wētāpunga that are part of its respiratory system.

AUTHOR'S NOTE

My cat used to bring me presents, and they were often wētā. Sometimes they were dead, but more often than not they were alive. I would have to work up the courage to somehow get them back into the garden without actually touching them. I didn't find this easy so decided to do some research about wētā to try and overcome my fears. The more I learned about this extraordinary creature, the more I came to appreciate them and see their beauty. I no longer look at them with fear but rather with awe and respect.

When I learned that some of the species were endangered (thankfully not the species my cat was bringing in), I felt very sad. The fact that we humans could be responsible for a creature no longer existing, when it has survived for all those millions of years, was terrible to me. I thought a book might help people of all ages get over their fears, too, and persuade them to try and save our weird and wonderful giant wētā. I hope this glimpse into the world of wētāpunga encourages children (and adults) to look deeper into things that might scare them at first.

I am not a wētāpunga expert, but this book has been fact-checked by many more knowledgable than me. Thank you to Delma O'Kane, Kaitakawaenga at Ngāti Manuhiri Settlement Trust for her cultural guidance. Thank you to Auckland Zoo ectotherm expert, Don McFarlane, and I am extremely grateful to him for giving the book the voice of authority it needs. Thank you also to Jane Healy, communications manager at Auckland Zoo, for all her advice and support. Thank you to Bateman Books, especially publisher Louise Russell, editor Sarah Yankelowitz and designer Jemma Moreira; and thank you to the very talented Laura Rayner for her delightful illustrations.

To find out more about this extraordinary arthropod, visit www.aucklandzoo.co.nz and www.doc.govt.nz.

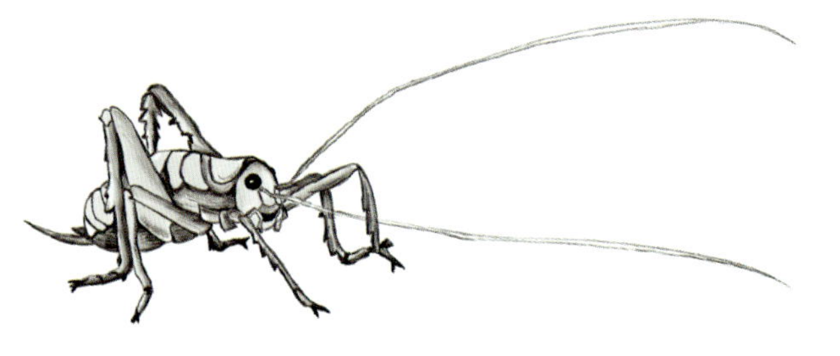

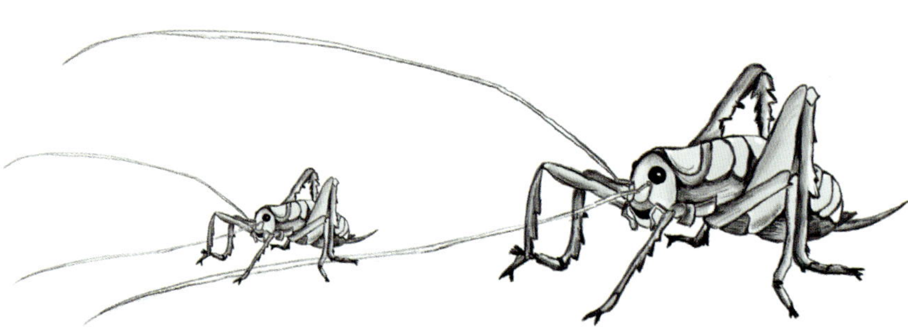

Wētāpunga

The biggest wētā in the world

Written by Jo van Dam
Illustrated by Laura Rayner

Keep an eye out for this wee beauty lurking throughout the book!

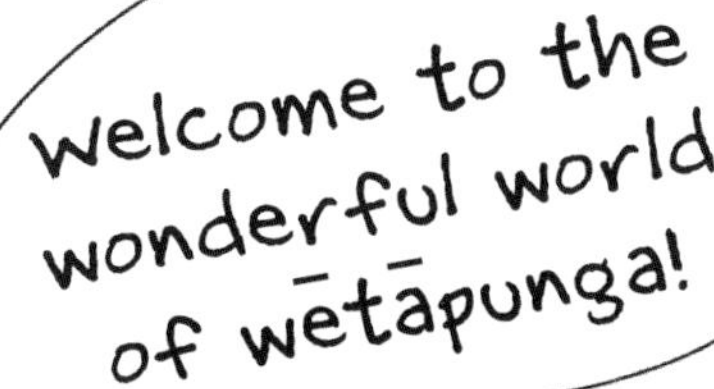

On Hauturu-o-Toi (Little Barrier Island), on a warm summer's evening around dusk, ectotherm keepers from Auckland Zoo are on the hunt for the largest species of giant wētā – wētāpunga.

Other animals are on the hunt, too.

Some animals want to eat wētāpunga.

The people want to save them.

Let's hope the people find them before the predators do . . .